LEARNING TO BREATHE

Also By Richard Stevenson

Driving Offensively (Sono Nis Press, 1985)

Suiting Up (Third Eye Publications, 1986)

Horizontal Hotel: A Nigerian Odyssey
(TSAR Publications, 1989)

Whatever It Is Plants Dream...
(Goose Lane Editions, 1990)

Learning
to
Breathe

POEMS BY

Richard Stevenson

CACANADADADA

Published by:

CACANADADADA PRESS LTD.
3350 West 21st Avenue
Vancouver, B.C. Canada
V6S 1G7

Set in Baskerville, 10½ pt on 11
Typesetting: The Typeworks, Vancouver, B.C.
Cover Design: Kirk Lawton
Cover Art: Alvin Jang

The publisher wishes to thank the Canada Council for its generous financial assistance.

Canadian Cataloguing in Publication Data

Stevenson, Richard, 1952-
    Learning to breathe

ISBN 0-921870-11-6

I. Title.
PS8587.T479L4   1992   C811'.54   C91-091708-6
PR9199.3.S73L4   1992

for my parents, Robert James
and Marguerite Stevenson,
with thanks for
the rich republic of childhood
they gave me...

ACKNOWLEDGEMENTS

Some of the poems in this collection have previously appeared in or been accepted for future issues of the following journals, small magazines, chapbooks, and anthologies:

Alpha Beat Soup, Ariel, Blue Buffalo, The Cacanadadada Review, Canadian Author & Bookman, Dick and Jane Have Sex (*Greensleeve Publications*, 1990), *d'VOID, Event, First Encounter, Grain, Great Canadian Murder and Mystery Stories* (*Quarry Press, 1991*), *Green's Magazine, K, North Dakota Quarterly, The Other Press Poetry Review, Pierian Spring, Prosepourri* (*Greensleeve Publications*, forthcoming), *SansCrit, Secrets From The Orange Couch, Skylines, White Wall Review, Words We Call Home: Celebrating Creative Writing At UBC* (Edited by Linda Svendsen, UBC Press, 1990), *Yak*, and *Zest*.

My thanks to the various editors for their support and encouragement, and to the Alberta Foundation for the Literary Arts and The Ontario Arts Council for grants which helped with living expenses during the writing of these poems.

Also, a big thank you to the members of the *Oldman River Writers Group*, and to Don McKay, John Donlan, Paddy O'Rourke, and Ronald Hatch for useful comments on the various versions of the manuscript of this book.

CONTENTS

III. THE RULE OF GRAVITY

I. ANOTHER HANSEL AND GRETEL STORY

THE LIZARD

The reptile and new brain are now
trying to make themselves visible.
                    — Robert Bly

Basking on a rock
in the chalkboard green
of late afternoon,

body pitted and scarred
as a dog-chewed plastic soldier
you might have left in the yard,

this alligator lizard's not
a particularly splendid specimen
an herpatologist might say;

but you're determined to catch it,
think of what a hit it will be
at Show and Tell come Monday.

Your shadow's black glove
glides glacially
before your outstretched arm —

freezes again as the skittish
lizard raises its blunt head,
poses, inquisitive, poised

as a querulous teacher
trying to pinpoint the source
of your impertinent noise.

And you watch its eyelids slide
sideways   like blackboard erasers
over inscrutable formulae;

you squint at ancient eyes
immutable as hornblende
in waterworn granite;

wonder what dark thoughts
stir in the limbic seats
behind their metamorphic gaze,

what Trojan horses
your own thoughts drag
behind their shadows

as memory beats
a retreat beneath
the outer eighth inch of your brain,

your hand's involuntary spasm
ejects the writhing rune
of terror's regenerable tail.

ANOTHER HANSEL AND GRETEL STORY

1. *Prologue*

Which summer is it, your tenth, eleventh?
I'm two years older, still young enough to
squeeze through the hole in the same fence.

Smell of juniper, a well-barbered hedge
gives way to rot, old rusty nails.
Oak leaves crackle like small autumn fires
beneath bare potatoes of elbows and knees.

We are brothers, goad each other through
more than elbows and knees of our old clothes.
Innocence by now is a scuffed pair of shoes;
the teacher's apple is both battered and bruised.

Cigarette butts litter the clearing. These
spent cartridges, fresh packs potent
as new ammunition. The nudie photos
wait, rolled up, in old mason jars.

Our fort's a dam of negative space
formed by beating back bush and thorns
into an igloo-shaped hollow, a place
in which to hide, lob words against

the terrible silence of smouldering desire.
We salute large breasts, men's stroke book
visions of split, dewy mons, resplendent
pink flesh, lace, garters, the very first

burning bush ever to spring
from light lovely lycra! Amazing!
Wondrous as any pink-eyed white rabbit
we ever flushed from that dark wood

or have hidden since, tamped back
into the glass jars, stuffed down
a threatening round barrel or hole.

2.

Strain your ears. Can you hear?
Upstairs. Mom and Dad making love.

The night is a dark cowl, a hood
we stretch over our furless backs.

Closer. The sound of our hearts
kicking like frightened rabbits
long held by the nape of the neck.

In our hands the bunched up sheets:
memories balled like Kleenex,
rubber bulbs we hold, squeeze
in the sweaty palms of our hands.

*

Go back further, turn thought infrared.
Catch the reclusive witch next door
bending over her smouldering couch.

Note the frantic, pale hand
scrabbling like a rodent smoked
out of her long coat sleeve.

See how she struggles
to beat out the long ash
that burrows deep into the pile.

Between her legs, rumour has it,
there once was a similar hole.
A girl her father could not flush out.

Now the tops of this old crone's nylons
swallow fat thighs the way two pythons
might swallow two transfixed little pigs.

What burned in her groin? What burnt out?
What bastard child, what deformed head
crowned there years ago no one must know.

3.

Death is a pet we bury in a shoe box,
a cross constructed of popsicle sticks
or an "x" of stones mother allows
to mark the spot in the back flower bed.
A brief respite in the ways of plastic soldiers
whose C.O. commands we disinter the bones.

Go back.
no skeletons; no bones.
Only crows, a flight of long days
with the last crumb of innocence in their
leader's beak. We fling handfuls of pebbles,
watch the crows circle back.
We pick up feathers, run fingers over them,
knit them together the way mother
does for us, always checking the zippers
of our worn, patched khaki corduroys.

Turtles, goldfish, hamsters, mice,
a canary once: all gone, buried like toys.
Evil's only an afterimage of a magazine
monster, projected in full-frontal spread,
a luminous skull of rumpled white sheets
at the foot of the bed.

4.

We see the old hag burning
tires in the backyard.
A black plume rises from
the burned-out bunkers
of her eyes.

It is a small town,
another country,
another time.

Each tire sends up sparks.
They flit like small birds
in the highest branches of the tree.

She is looking out from a dark wood
to where her village once stood.
Her head sits like an owl, grips
the branch of an old oak.

Any moment now mice will
emerge from the rubble,
skitter into the clearing.

Talons will find fur
as the five tines of her fork
stir through the ash.

5.

Ten or eleven. Memory a long line
of breadcrumbs through the dark woods.
Dog-chewed plastic soldiers, dinky toys
surface where bones might have been.
It is difficult to remember the time scheme.
Movies: *Pork Chop Hill* and *The Longest Day*
envelop us, extend their blue pseudopodia
from the T.V. screen, our family's four walls.

A world of sin opens like some huge
sweet-smelling carnivorous plant.
Drowsy as bees caught in the sugar
of pop bottles we leave all day
on the front porch, we fall into it.
Become heroes and rogues both
anxious to try out the television roles.

Conscience is a lid we punch nail holes in.
Clap over the jar of the old lady's back yard
so she can breathe while we watch
her climb the glass sides of her own life.

                    *

Now it is not *The Munsters, The Addams Family*
we hold up to the light; not a drowsy insect
careening around the narrow lip of a bottle
we see, but a father and daughter falling
over each other like bugs at the bottom of a jar.

                    *

NO SOLICITORS, NO PEDLARS, NO NOTHING:
yellow paper affixed to the front door
by the big-headed thumbtacks of our eyes.
Which Halloween is it? The paper curls
like a dog's upper lip. Words scratch:
a German Shepherd behind a thin door.
We knock, knock again because the old lady
will mutter and curse quite audibly,
but will never, ever open the door.

6.

Ritual demands a trip to the barn,
and so we must go there, one at a time.
If not to see what hangs from the rafters,
then to see the empty cages stacked high.

This, while the old woman is home,
we have witnesses who have been,
know the surge of long grass, rush
and kiss of flames at the heels.

This, while the moon is full, plump
as any white chicken in the hand of a geek,
or when it is thin, milky and
melts like wafer under the tongue.

*

A dead cat lies on a barrel:
curled, furless humunculus with
skin pulled thin as rice paper
over its foetal-bowed bones.

We lift it with a stick,
watch the maggots fall gentle
as rain drops from the full
eaves of its weathered ribs.

*

Think now: was there
ever a foetus miscarried,
buried in the basement?
Could incest ever be uglier

than the rumour we let
past the white picket fence
of our perfect teeth?
Turn the cat over again.

7.

Lift the receiver,
the sound of the old bat's breathing
scurries like rats
single file down the wire.

Silence: an invisible,
colourless gas
tumbles from air vents,
seeps under the sash.

A huge darkness with
its sack of light
laughs up the chimney,
grins under doors.

Gather brown flowers
from parks and boulevards.
Add water and stir
in a black patent purse.

Curse and jump the fence when
she comes at you with her car.
Yell across the years
your abject apologies.

Tell her you really
like her cookies
and you're truly sorry
for nibbling at her walls.

Pass her the hard,
brittle bones of your words;
tell her, if you can;
you're fat enough now.

8. *Epilogue*

And what of this gingerbread house?
After age and realtors come to call:
isn't there a sausage machine after all?
Do words not break our bones
to make their bread? Are lice
not crawling in her hair?
You stand and stare, and still
the words like moths eat
holes in the closet of old coats
that hang in open air.

Chicken bones are piled in a pyramid
in one corner of the livingroom floor.
Mouse turds tumble from all the cupboards.
Basin, tub, and tile turn the colour of autumn leaves.
Aquariums grow greener than the eyes of cats.
Chickens in canary cages look fatter than the day.
Are there no children in the oven then?

Your feet go through the floorboards
in all the basement rooms.
Where do we go then? What do we do
when all the words we speak are pieces of bread
torn from the same loaf; all the words we've spoken
are fat black birds that eat our way home?

SOFT DIET

Every morning the same sad song
over the kitchen radio:
"At Beneficial — boop boop —
you're good for more.
At Beneficial — boop boop —
you're good for more."

Father drags the razor along his jaw,
trowels away the shadow and foam:
so much mortar between the
hard edges of the things he sees.

Mother butters his toast
and cooks him two eggs
while we loll like accident victims
until the third time we're called.

The car heats up its black notes,
wedding one molecule of carbon
to one of oxygen, while the sun's infusion
seeps through the lateral slats in the fence.

Today his eggs will be vulcanized.
Mother's competency in the kitchen
will come under heavy fire.
the words' shrapnel will reach our ears.

We'll get up when he's gone,
go to school with the same
metal taste on our tongues.
Three apples in our lunch kits
guttering under the short
fuses that lit them to begin with.

There to be taught that a noun
is a part of speech you can eat,
while on the other side of the world
a set of dentures falls to the
bottom of a very tall glass.

FALLING DOWN AND GETTING UP AGAIN

In a park in your neighbourhood
children slide like little
gumdrops out of their pants.
Big boys you know by name
hold them by their belt loops,
dump them onto the ground.

They run around the park
like cherubim, all pink buns,
split pears, and mushroom buds.
The big boys pat their bottoms
and send them running after you.

Soon they will get to play
walkie talkie in the woods.
Talk into the big boys'
pretend microphones.
This will be more fun than
running under the sprinkler.
More fun than eating popsicles.

The big boys you know
will make them naughty,
threaten to tell their Moms.
They will have pictures
of them all — having fun.
Doing naughty fun things
Mommy and Daddy do not do.

Better not to tell them.
Better to keep a secret,
even when fun stops being fun.
Doing fun things can take
some getting used to.
Like riding bikes.
Falling. Getting up again.

HENRY, IN MID-LEAP

"Henry Lee has lost his wits.
Henry sucks his mother's tits,"
we kids would yell
until this hairy, gentle man
would take the bait and give chase,
run, shambling, ape-like, after us.

We would jump across a ditch
and he, faithful as a family dog,
would follow. Back and forth.
KA-nip KA-nop, a pingpong ball.
We would laugh; he would laugh.

So loving and trusting and gullible,
he'd do it for hours if we let him
or he didn't fall in and get soaked.
For Henry Lee *had* lost his wits,
and his mother *did* love him so.

She'd call him for supper, and he
would come. A perfect loving son.
That is, until his mother died
and something of Henry broke inside.
Then he wouldn't let the girls touch
his big, hairy thing, or play with it.

Then there was no one left
to wind him up, take his hand,
or point his purple pecker home.
No relatives. No friends.
Just some men who were nice once
and gave him a ride in their van.

They took him to their castle-on-a-hill;
he escaped and found a bigger ditch —
a river wide enough and deep enough
to take him home. And Henry jumped
into a blue and cloudless morning,
believing he would catch us,
finally, on the other side.

STEALING THIRD

Nothing below the waist.
That is the rule.

Right hand draped around
the soft curve of her shoulder,
left unbuttoning her blouse;

dizzy from the Olympian heights
and wet evenings in Paris
behind her ears;

I'm safe on second base,
eyes cocky as a pro-league pitcher's
staring down from her mounds;

watch her eyes,
distracted players,
move out to center field.

The sun is a ball
hit high over the fence,
out of the park —

I'm Little Jack Horner
in a corner
in a dugout
in the dark —

Hear a voice in the bleachers
cheer me on,
moan " I love you..., "

as my fingers lead off
beneath the elastic
waistband of her underpants.

No foul.
My hand races to
tag the base,

the ball still
in the air somewhere,
the bases loaded.

COLQUITZ CREEK IMPROVEMENT PROJECT

1. Sectioned Like An Orange

Winter: thoughts stall around
each page of the calendar,
a dent in the fender of the car ahead.

Mud on the windshield or
blood under a microscope:
so many days bottled in eyes
and thermoses, lunch boxes
with the sun inside
sectioned like an orange:
we park our cars each day until four.

Sky has a hide as thick as that
of a full grown elephant
and when the moon comes
it lopes through the shadows of trees
like a wounded animal
shot through with a ball
of our brains.

Eight o'clock sharp we fall
out of our cars: entrails
fed piecemeal to the shadows
barking at our feet.

The foreman brings instructions,
whistle, and a bag of peanuts.

He plants them,
presupposing for the sake of art
he has an audience.
All the trees smile
a row of perfect teeth.

2. *Job Security (for Tom Wayman)*

This is John's third Local Initiatives job.
Digging holes, filling them, moving them over
is something he's obviously good at by now.

Ex-postie, he sorts and slots trees with aplomb,
fir and cedar saplings lined up neatly,
planted in tall grass at the brow of the hill —

just inside the reach of the grass crew's
gang mower blades, of course. And why not?
That's "job security," after all. "The buggers

won't water 'em anyway, you wait and see."
One gumboot drifts the shovel blade home;
he pulls the stick shift of the handle back.

"See. A perfect wedge every time. No sweat."
Snicks each tree like a bullet into the breach,
closes the gap either side with his other heel.

"Give 'em a forty-five degree stomp your side,
they'll stand up straight as long as it takes
for the boys on Permanent to give them a shave.

One other thing: don't wear new clothes.
The only thing that should be green is your hat.
Keep that on. Motor like a mallard when the boss is around."

3. *Auguries and Hijinks*

His best Mae West impression yet:
"Save up your nickels and your dimes
and come and see me sometime":

green hardhat a rakish beret;
sexy grin, gumboots, and slicker;
a frozen racoon draped round his neck.

He twirls the tail, slinks through the bush,
right hand on hip, wagging his ass
in imitation of her infamous style.

Runs through his vaudeville routine. We laugh,
build a funeral pyre out of brush, grass,
old tires and garbage dragged from the creek.

It's enough to squeak us through another day,
watching the whiskers curl back from the flames
like some Old World colonel's waxed moustache.

Enough theatre to warrant the cost of admission
to these ranks of disenfranchised, misemployed.
The water's high enough to hide the winter props,

and so we flick the steel belts of the tires
back into the creek. Come back tomorrow
to catch another gumboot fish, another dollar.

The greenbacks affix themselves to the sky
like lampreys or remoras: leaves caught
on the bowed branches of deciduous trees.

We spread our boots above the heat registers,
watch them dry slowly, steam rising like smoke —
hickory smoke from old treaty salmon, indentured flesh.

4. *Outer Rings*

The idea is to clear the creek
so the fish can come up to spawn —
not that any self-respecting salmon
would choose this particular route,
let alone nudge noses with old rubber boots.

Nothing leaps here but adolescent hormones,
and even then the exchange of fluids here
amounts to little more than a pit stop:
"Blow jobs: five bucks, horizontals: ten,"
if the junior high graffiti is to be believed.

But even graffiti loses impact to the rain,
decaying masonry. We shore up the path,
pour pea gravel and asphalt, each day
the sun rising, falling precise as a tonearm
into the same worn groove, same sad song:

"Put your hairy snake in my hairy hole."
Today's sleaze merely the flip side
of yesterday's sentimental lies.
A way of keeping a hula hoop of truth
spinning to the same platter moon.

Makin' the bacon at work or play,
saying something stupid about a need
that runs like bicycle tires through hot
steaming ground: asphalt or flesh.
Telling the truth, but telling it slant:

I was here. I made love to someone.
He/ she loved me too, and our names
grew with the tree we carved them in.
Fish thrashed in the current we made,
have jumped every hoop every year since.

CONDOM TALES

1.

Times were so tough Wes used to wash out his condoms with a toothbrush, hang them right there on the clothesline next to Sylvia's re-usable pads. "Party hats" he called them when the neighbours' kids would ask what they were, or "toques for the Pope's nose." Then snapped, "Now mind your business and go home."

2.

The safe machine in the Dominion Hotel john offered a rainbow of colours to choose from, might have been a gumball machine, or so it must have seemed to some wise kid who etched "This gum tastes like rubber" next to the crack "Break one and win a baby!"

3.

"Gossamer thin and smooth as silk" the label on the box used to read, meaning, I suppose, you'd scarcely notice the condom once it was on; but no: we noticed, and more than once withdrew with the pope wearing a droopish toque, or, like Tom Terrific, went toot toot and blew a hole in the hat out of which issued great gouts of smoke that somehow indicated we'd got the idea, and hoped the ardent little spermatazoa would somehow fag out before they swam the channel and not get to shake the mayor's hand while the sunburst of fallopian fireworks gave back delayed rumbles to our ears.

4.

And somewhere I read of a male pill. Developed and tested. Piloted years ago by willing inmates with high libidos and little to do but wank in a tube. It got the sperm count down all right; was abandoned nonetheless. Marketing problems: it didn't sit well with alcohol, apparently, and so would never sell. The male body its own highball; so now we're just waiting for something to float the olives, while we twiddle, fiddle with the swizel sticks.

5.

Talk like brother plumbers of fittings and valves. Vasect-omies seemed like such a good idea—so easy to work on outside plumbing and never mind what was hidden behind the drywall. The faucets and fittings were so well installed. We were pleased with the aesthetic of a single spout. Now we're back to re-plumbing our women too.

6.

In order to purchase his first condom, my brother had to buy one comb, one toothbrush, a bottle of aftershave, pay tax twice, and return to the counter ten minutes after the large-breasted woman in Pharmacy was gone. Once he had the box of condoms in his hand, and, seeing our father in nearby Stationery, had to ditch it on a shelf of shampoo. All this at a time when my younger cousin bought 12-cent comic books one at a time so he wouldn't have to pay the one penny tax.

So with the economics of sex. You had to make it with some-one. But that someone had to appear to be a part of the weekly grocery bill: an item under Sundries. Love came in disposable lots. Something like the funny papers on Sundays: useful after-ward for wrapping fish heads before we took them to the gar-bage cans.

7.

The pill made it as easy for the man as putting coins in a park-ing meter, and gave us all a meter to feed. Most of the women I went out with before I married were on it; making love to-gether, we could almost hear the click click click of the biologi-cal clocks moving the needle in a clean sweep across the dial of our eyes. So hungry for whatever coin we could give each other. Ultimately, one or the other of us would run out of spare change.

After thirty, our women tell us, there is nowhere to park your desire on the street. Everyone is circling the same few blocks. Looking for the perfect slot: one block from dinner and as close to the theatre as possible.

8.

Now it could cost a man or a woman his or her life to have sex together. We wear them out of respect — something like dark clothes at a funeral, or asbestos suits in a house fire.

9.

Some say the sexual revolution is dead. The singles bar has ac-quired the ambience of a church social, complete with little sandwiches. We all must take little bites, recite a new catechism of need. Confess indiscretions of the flesh.

Everywhere the lovers are breaking out hats. Placing them like serviettes next to the table. It's going to be a long feast or a famine. It's time to draw up our chairs and say grace. Get ready for the rich feast of binomials of genus and species. Set out the cutlery for loaves and fishes all over again.

10.

Someone should invent industrial strength condoms. Condoms built to last: prophalactics with ziplocs that double as freezer bags. That way we might save ourselves from what we've become. We could approach each other from inside special gloves. Stay the radioactive isotope of love.

WRECK BEACH, VANCOUVER

Much too cool to strut in the buff,
however brassy and brazen the sky
in doffing its own grey winter clothes,
yet the die-hards will not be daunted.

Jaunty in sunglasses and pullover sweaters,
they doff their drawers, let the bellclappers
of their better halves bang blue matins
between their knees, their nuts shrunk

up to their groins, hard as green berries:
to walk their prize peters the way
the rich trail after pedigree poodles,
troll for approval all down the beach.

Later, firm or pendulous of belly or breasts,
spartan or hairy, dingled or donged,
every bush will burn with the light
that averts all eyes to novels and dogs.

Such is God's image: a tangle of snakes;
Perseus wears mirrors and Ms. Medusa flakes.

WALKMAN BLUES

'I'll buy you new clothes; you'll live in a big house and go to the best schools. I'll give you everything money can buy and you'll be happy, happy, happy!''

—John Boles speaks to Shirley Temple in Curly Top (1937)

Apple Annie's all grown up
and happy happy happy.
Her analyst helped her
join the dots her freckles made;
now she's joined the Red Brigade.

Holistic Harry's happy too
with his backpack and microbus,
his new life in sweats and jogging shoes.
Without his wife and children,
he knows what to do.

Jack and Jill went down the hill,
fetching moonbeams in a bucket;
dropped pretense with their pants,
unwound, got down,
lived happily in their laughter.

Then Jack's stock fell down,
Jill's baby crowned,
the eighties careened around the corner
of Primal Scream, T.M., and est;
they bought an RV and moved West.

Now Jack has priorized his goals,
walks the strand in Kitsilano,
metal detector in hand,
while Jill, in Spandex, combs the shoals
for burls to make table lamps.

We're all happy happy happy,
fat, crow-foot runneled, and grey;
where we're at is where the cellular phone
in the runabout we strapped to the roof racks
said we'd be, or the message found us —

after the beep, somewhere ahead of the long dash
and before two seconds of silence.
Where the moon's ringing, jumping off the hook,
and the gods' smarmy receivers
are snuggled at everyone's ears.

II. THE WORLD
ACCORDING TO REUTER

THE WORLD ACCORDING TO REUTER

In Kigali, the capital of Rwanda,
government officials have announced
the official bride price will be
three hoes instead of the traditional cow.

Mothers with daughters of marriageable age
are outraged and claim, indignantly,
this devalues the worth of a young girl to
less than the price of a basket of bananas.

Yet more injurious than the blow
to the haughty parents' pride
is the considerable loss in carrying charges,
the attack on small business growth.

Some fathers have been known to command
100,000 Rwandan francs (about $1,640)
for making the beast with two backs
spit out the right genetic code —

and there is no denying they work at it.
Like zealous patrons at the slot machines
in Vegas or Maseru or Macao,
they pump their women full of small change.

Until three sour lemons light up their eyes
and the women spill forth babies! babies!
Babies that become sons with strong wills;
babies that become daughters with strong backs.

And while many young people approve
of reducing the bride price to a nominal gift,
the stalwarts of the ruling National Revolutionary
Movement for Development party strongly object.

They would as soon move cows, move their bowels
as cave in to the practice of tilling their
daughters' wombs for the price of a few hoes.
Their minds slam shut cash register drawers.

Development or no development, it is the will
of the village men to keep producing children.
If it is hoes they will get for their pains, O.K.
Let there be daughters. Let there be hoes.

THE VENDORS

It is late. Branches begin to stir,
dandle shadows heavy as ripe mangoes
twisting on the last gibbets of light.

Each wall of white-washed adobe
drags the bum leg of the hour
behind it, lurches down streets

while the people's god pauses,
pulls the sky's fob out each day
to look at the dial, pocket it again.

There is going to be a speech. The Colonel
leads the rich corpuscular motorcade of
party hopefuls along the rutted, dusty track.

Already the vendors are busy setting up
the dark, fetid pyramid of heads,
plumping the ruffled leaves of the facts,

so that when he gets to the podium
he will be able to mop up any questions
along with the beads of sweat from his forehead,

crumple them into the white-knuckled tubers
of his fist. And the produce will keep
until the vendors come again to exfoliate

the rotten outer leaves of their metal fruit,
lay a red wash over the walls and the streets,
throw words like spades full of earth

over the smashed melons, fly-blown meat,
until the eyes of the aged collapse,
their bruised fruit of hope invaginates.

Lies preserve the candied legs of words
like insects in amber, while silence rests
its wet burlap over dessicated vegetables.

A SOAP CALLED VICTORY

"Ads for soap, the one commodity even the poorest slum dweller will buy, are omnipresent in the media. The two major brands, People and Victory, engage in perpetual psychological warfare over the airwaves. Housewives march across the tube with banners for their favorite soap, chanting 'Peo-ple! Peo-ple!' Among the hovels of refugees who have fled to the city from the war without end in the countryside, a triumphant radio voice blares day and night 'I have Victory in my hands!'"

— Sara Miles in an article on El Salvador in *Mother Jones*

I have Victory on my hands now,
work up the suds into a lather.
Nothing foments a heady romance
quite like the smell of Victory.

I think maybe my hands will come clean.

People soap is much more plebeian.
You can drop a bar into a reservoir
and one hand will not notice
what the other hand is doing.

Two hands, as in prayer,
can make neither come clean.

Victory soap is so much better.
Victory soap smells so much fresher.
Victory removes gun grease, sweat,
even the twin stains of suspicion and fear.

With Victory on my hands
I can almost forget
the dirt under my feet.

POEM AFTER A PHOTOGRAPH IN *MOTHER JONES*

So peaceful seem the severed heads,
so relaxed, so calm the almond eyes,
the pocked and blood-smeared cheeks;
so peaceful as to seem asleep,
to have dreamed themselves that way.

Any day the wind might blow,
riffle through the black fields
of their luxuriant, full-bodied hair,
and lift them from this abattoir soft
as soap bubbles from a child's breath,

and they will float for a while,
drift above the stippled stalk
of God's ragged dandelion clock,
settle, one by one, on El Salvador's
blood-engorged soil and sand.

They will send down roots that grow new
bodies whose arms and legs are safer
than the ones they remember having before,
bodies eye-deep in earth and blood
whose skulls grow nondescript as stones.

THE KILLING FIELDS OF UGANDA

In the lovely green fields of Uganda
the children flock like lambs,
gambol over discarded car springs,
pangas used to crack their skulls.

It doesn't matter who cracks the whip now —
Milton Obote, Idi Amin Dada —
the syllables of the rulers' names
are still as the stones on their tongues.

They are white now. White enough
that we in the West can look at them
and wonder where the yellow went,
if they brushed their teeth with Pepsodent.

So white we can pick them up
like seashells on a pleasant beach at home,
or hold them by their hollow orbits
and admire them like *objets d'art* —

expensive vases, say. Even admire
their heft and weight the way
we admire a new bowling ball,
the way it travels down a lane.

So white they don't need to ask for foreign aid,
but merely whisper of the wind
that tousles the tall green grass around them,
repeat Victoria, Victoria in the riffles on her lake.

So white even the black museum curators at Makindye
gather their bones like firewood of ancient days
and stack their skulls like cannon balls
outside the former Research Bureau in Kampala.

So white and free of skin and tendon
they smile like the thwacked slice in a golfball
and travel twice as far when the right
angle of iron addresses them.

PORTRAIT OF A TORTURER

You must believe what I say. I am a refugee, a victim too. What I did, I did out of fear — fear for my own life, fear of reprisals. It was either them or me, my family. I didn't want to hurt anyone — not at first, at least. You must believe me.

Murder made me sick, physically ill; torture gave me nightmares; I couldn't sleep.

Still, it was better to come in the night — to take the whole family at once, you see. No one was left to suffer that way. No pair of eyes could look at me and know. Better that babies be thrown in the air and skewered on bayonets or have their brains dashed out quickly against a rock or a wall.

They could not grow up to bear arms that way.

They would not have to suffer poverty, disease.

Better to toss the enemy out of a plane — watch them grow small like the blue dot on your black and white T.V. when the monitor is turned off. It is an easy death, much less unpleasant than bashing in skulls with a rifle butt, having to pick up the brains, mop up the blood.

If you're lucky the jungle or ocean swallows them up. No smell assails your nostrils before the vultures or animals pick the bones clean. The ocean is endless and deep. Nothing that lands there can seep back into the water table; there is only the tide to bring back a body.

By then it is bloated and soft, not a person at all.

These corpses terrorize and demoralize the enemy.

Captives that die before we are ready for them to die clandestinely in faraway places. It is unfortunate and messy sometimes to dispose of these. I found it easiest to leave them a few days, blanch them with boiling water so their faces came away cleanly when I peeled their skin.

Acid always worked in a pinch.

If you didn't look, you didn't see a face.

None of these things were pleasant, of course — least of all torturing the enemy first. Their screams are unnerving. I couldn't do it at first, but then my superiors told me they could always find someone to trade places with me. Invited me to consider the prisoners' lot. Invited me to choose which side I was on.

So I started with beatings — first the bottoms of their feet; eventually, their ribs, faces.

I got so I could break bone.

The electrodes and acid, the rubber necklace and *pau-de-arara*, the mind drugs came later.

It wasn't that I ever became immune to what I had to do. You must believe that. I didn't. I often had dreams, nightmares — faces haunt me even now. Even here in your country. Screams and bullets ricochet in my head.

I am not dead, you understand. I am alive.

I am human just as you are.

I feel their pain and mine. You understand? I had to think of my family first — what they would do if I refused to comply. It isn't easy to escape. Not ever. Members of the militia can't just disappear. I was a career soldier since I was fifteen. The face I wore on the street was never my own. I was well-known. I would be missed.

It's always easier if you cannot be missed.

AMNESTY REPORT

Dusk. The sun still cooks
bodies broken like eggs
on deserted back lots.
Shadows arch their backs,
stretch, hook their claws
into the lush, green pile
of new suburban lawns.

On the porch a family
poses for a photograph
out of *Better Homes and Gardens*:
husband: handsome, broad-shouldered,
wife: slender and petite,
children: spiky-haired, squat
as grocery-aisle pineapples.

The timer is set, the landscape
wavers like wallpaper
seen through the heatwaves
of a four-slice toaster deluxe.
Who would ever suspect that
people like these would disappear?

Yet already you can detect
a small glimmer of unease
as the girls look outside the frame,
the mother frowns, her trim waist
cinched in by the belt, belled
skirt of nineteen-fifties fashion
hourglass through which her body pours.

The smiling, friendly neighbour
is getting set to turn informer.
Of what, on whom is anybody's guess.
He pulls and pulls at the cord
of his new gas-powered mower,
uproots silence, words, reason
like old turnips from the ground.

He is only minding his turf, you say?
Only walking the perimeter of his lot?
Yes, it is true. I fully agree.
He is walking in circles, is
entertaining a green thought
whose perimeter is ever-decreasing;
ambles through a wide swath of love.

BEIJING MASSACRE

To be in Tiananmen Square that day
was to be one drone in a hive of bees,
one leaf shaking, bending away
from a strong headwind in a tree.

The country lay still as a man
with bees in his beard,
until the bees became beard,
the beard a single cluster of bees
gathered around a pheromone
of hope and of fear.

The country became one man
covered from head to foot
in a cluster of bees,
the one man's thought
devoted to the idea
of learning, once again,
how to breathe.

And the bees' one thought:
how to breathe with him,
how to collapse and swell
like a bellows to feed
one man the oxygen he needs.

How to retain the shape of the man
when the man's body depends
like a ripe plum from the tree.

When what a plum wants,
with all its being,
with the fullness of time,
is to ripen, to fall,
and be eaten.

When all it needs
is the heat of the sun
and a little gravity,
one mouth to open,
to say "plum"
once, perfectly,
and taste it
on its tongue.

KUNG FU MOVIE, NGURU

Friday and Sunday nights in Nguru
the people come in droves to fill
the plastic chairs and wooden seats
of this cracked cement amphitheatre
that serves as the only cinema here.

The audience is mostly Moslem and
composed of young men and boys,
weekend escapees from the Government
Girls' Secondary School, a few
Filipinos and white contract expats.

Nigeria being the regular stage,
reality is confined to the streets.
B-movie dusters, American gumshoe,
Indian romance, and Kung Fu movies
hold undisputed sway here.

They love to see Bruce Lee
or anyone with half-slanted eyes
kick the ions out of the air,
and practice in the parking lot
high kicks and karate chops.

Tonight the plot is simple enough
for even a whiteman to understand:
the villagers' market is pillaged
by highland thieves. Bruce Lee and Co.
kick shit through the hierarchy.

No one ducks out, even for a piss —
there's plenty of sand up front
between the first row and screen for this,
and when they squat on their heels,
the viewers' rigas provide the privacy.

So tonight the visible enemy gets theirs —
never mind meningitus and the dastardly
invisible furies the harmattan brings
by raising the feces and dust. Tonight
a white horse in full regalia rides
the skies; heaven's a silver screen.

                    Nguru, Nigeria

A LONG-HANDLED BROOM
LABELLED "FOR COBWEBS ONLY"

Between the valence and the walls,
the windows and mosquito screens,
wherever a belay of space is gained,
pitons of light betray visibility,
spiders rappel themselves and weave
a web of clean deceit and sophistry.

This one's doing push-ups above an old corpse,
that one sips daintily: is on a first date.
Boris here hangs like a warm, wrinkled
scrotum in his cotton swaddling,
twitches only when the currents change
or a fly, like a butler, pulls the bell cord.

A large fly zooms about the room,
eventually blunders into the trap:
a small buzz in territorial air space —
nothing a post, a good sturdy rope,
a bag over the head cannot contain.
Even hope can be made to collapse like a straw.

I think of all the wattled jowls that wagged
before the O.A.U.* tanks rolled into Chad;
recall how the refugees and thieves came down
to Maiduguri like the baby spiders I'll chase
the moment I lift the broom to these hangers-on,
and my eyes cannot pull up their own tent pegs.

* *Organization of African Unity*

54

ZAVIN

The woman of Zavin's dreams
is an Armenian peasant girl,
a virgin in her early twenties
who dreams of children first
and serving her husband last.

She must be Armenian, he says,
because the Turks all but
decimated his people; and, preferably,
have high, firm breasts and wide hips,
so she can bear babies and hard work.

Zavin is Christian and Lebanese,
once danced to Kalashnikovs
and the disco beat of Beirut
before a bullet sent him packing
to West Africa, Muslim Maiduguri.

Now he lives with Shafik and Rafik,
works for a steel and engineering firm.
Enjoys fast women and fast cars,
imported Lebanese food, belly dancers,
and a glass of Arack by the pool.

And right now there is this mongrel bitch
on a snout cruise among the garbage heaps.
He bears down on it full throttle,
dodging deep puddles, broken engine blocks
along the narrow shanty streets of Bolori.

He takes pleasure in seeing our faces blanch
as he veers at the last second or grazes
a piteous yelp out of its accordion ribs,
aims to get closer to the skittish life
and frayed wires of the life he left behind.

Armenian then. As passionate as Zavin is
about wanting to learn English; as resourceful
and tenacious as these thorn trees that fight
like black whores over the purse of the moon.
A woman he can spend his bullets in forever, amen.

III. THE RULE OF GRAVITY

THE CLIFFORD OLSON KILLINGS

1. *Clifford Olson*

They pay me so much a head.
I take them to the bodies,
unearth their desires.

They want to know how and when
each victim was killed,
what kind of twisted will
could find pleasure in their pain —

What kind of rage could
build to such a storm inside me
and leave the red bicycle of my heart
propped so quiet, so still, against
a back wall of a store for so long.

I walk down a long red hall
and see all the faces of
all the families, all the children
smiling safely under glass.

I would reduce the world
to two dimensions if I could.
"Beautiful to look at, beautiful to hold,
but if you break it, consider it sold"
the sign in the china shop says.

I bring the bull into the shop,
begin serious bidding
on the length of his chain.
Someone has to pay for the damage
or there will be more, much more.

Your sons and your daughters
come out to play. Ride their bikes
or walk past the Safeway
to put their quarters in the willing
slots of multi-orgasmic machines.

I give them beer. Rides. L.S.D.
They boldly go where they've never been.
And when I tell them to bend over,
a green light flashes on in my head.

Bing. Bing. Bing. My circuits
run amok with Pacmen and Ghosts.
I can't let them win, don't you see?
I keep racking up numbers,
trying to win a free game.

I break skulls to break even.
The long shaft in my eyes
is spring-loaded, releases
the steel ball of the moon
to bounce off every baffle and paddle,
scoot down spread cheeks and thighs.

Count the holes. Fillings in their teeth.
Note the striations where muscle
once attached itself to bone.
Examine their flayed viscera
under the strong lights of reason and hope.

Re-solder the frayed ends of my words,
trace back the switches that
tripped my horrible need.
Match the colour-coded wires,
see where they lead.

Names, dates, places: join up the dots.
Empty my pockets, my mind's bottom drawer
writhing with snakes,
snails, and puppy dog tails
that make me your monster.

When you draw close, I shrink back,
my skin viscous, soft, palpable —
a snail's. My words' antennae
retract. I leave silver patinas
on the trails. Truth
hangs on the edge of each leaf.

Bodies moulder elsewhere. How many
and how soon I send up their names
like soul kites or soap bubbles
remains my affair. What facts put back
are not the soul's works-in-a-drawer.

And so I keep you hanging while you
hold me in the clean white hanky
of your jurisprudence and cells,
hum like a dial tone or whine
like a receiver held too long
away from the hunkering black phone.

You see, no one stays stiff forever,
not even the dead. Nor any part,
not even a finger, wherever
it's pointed: I smile, swim past
the sweet peach of its glans.

Be thankful then your daughters
are dead and not pregnant.
The nail in the head
is just another cock.

Be thankful you weren't home
when I came and knocked.
At the end of a long red hall
is a door, another hymen
I have to break.

Wrap the money round your finger then.
Go ahead. Slide me a bone.
I'm willing and of age.
You know I'm available:
I'm always home.

2. *The Bereaved,*
To Judge and Jury

for Don Sullivan
& The Victims of Violence

We are the victims that won't go away.
Our sons and daughters are dead:
they are no problem now; they are O.K.
Safely consigned to a plot and a file,
their precise trajectory from here
is patently clear.

They have gone to "a better place,"
can reclaim their innocence the way
you reclaim your coats and hats
after the final act of some poignant play.

"Unfortunate incidents" end, after all,
and the dead have their place in a plot:
verisimilitude requires they stop
talking when they meet a bullet or knife.

Yet there is no place to put us,
no hole or keep; no file, no furnace,
no urn, and no grave.
Columns of print that might fit on a stone
contain no gutters to catch the flow
of our blood in a convenient basin or bowl.

No arrest, no arraignment, no conviction —
even for murder in the first degree —
can snick home the bullet of our hate,
and no hair trigger of chapter and verse
can riddle the killer with enough holes
to let through the sun.
Our day is done.

We bury your mistakes;
you send us the funeral bills.
And when the killer
sues us for guardianship
of the remaining undead:
our children — the ones we
have left to love and console —
you pay the killer's legal fees,
issue a shovel so he can dig
a deeper hole for our grief.

Throw in the first spade-full of earth then,
while we stick
like unwanted clay to the shovel
or fall away like grains of sand,
fill the bottom of that legal hourglass
the blind impartial mistress of justice
holds in one hand.
Then tip her on her back,
fill her with enough seed to right
that hourglass waist of hers;
put justice back on two glass feet
that never reach the floor.

We are the victims that can't go away.
Even now we are falling through space
to a portal wider than the widest pupil
of the blackest, coldest eye.
The killer appraises us.
We are his; our bodies
are circumscribed and defined:
We are the most readily attainable,
the most bountiful, desireable
real estate this side of the grave.

3. *Clifford Olson,*
From The Kingston Pen

It isn't enough
that I killed your children,
that they came to me willingly
on the simplest of pretexts
and begged for their lives.

It isn't enough
that they took off their clothes,
shivered and whimpered and cried
while I split their vaginas and cheeks
like the sections of a ripe orange,

that my rage detonated a payload
that destroyed avenues and streets
inside *you* they'd never call home,
or that the last quivers
of their sphincters
accompanied a paroxysm of joy
in my groin.

It isn't enough
that they shit their pants,
that their eyes roll and tongues loll
and I hold a rich bouquet
of strangled orchids in my hands.

It isn't enough
that I get paid
for the white blooms
of all the faces
that open before their graves,
that I siphon off
the blood of all
the blanched,
broken, and bereaved
that weep openly on the news.

I must fit snugly into you:
a bullet in the breach
of your uneasy love.
Open up whole boutonnieres of blood
on all the starched blue tunics
of all your uniforms.

I am writing to say
you haven't heard the last of me.
My letters to you Moms and Dads
are crusted with my sinful seed.

Blood rises to my glans
the way mercury
stands in a thermometer.
Right now I'm hot.
My pecker stands
like a fireman in his red hat,
poised under the peaked roof
of the book in your lap.

4. *The Victims of Sexual Crime*

We are the dead.
Our photographs:
quick, shallow graves
your eyes tamp down
when you turn the page.

Arrayed like gravestones,
our milk teeth take
their solemn place
in this cackling hole
of old victims' bones.

No longer naive,
we smile at the camera
that would swallow us
one at a time
like peas off a fork.

Deaf, dumb, and blind,
we stare back from
cataracts of print.

Beseech you to pray,
to hang on to the life that
falls like a spade full of earth
through both of your eyes.

Our faces? Merely helpmates —
like Demosthenes' stones;
we shift, roll under the
quickening tongue of light.

5. *The Police, To John Q. Public*

We *know* you are outraged;
we are outraged ourselves.

Outraged the defense would
bow to the will of such
a creature as he.

Outraged they should stoop
to the stooly's old game
of paying for info.

Let alone pay
ten grand a body,
an unconscionable fee.

And, yes, we agree
the money should have been a ruse
from the beginning, bait to trap

a monster that should never ever
have been free in the first place.
We object to paying for the cage!

But the law is the law,
justice, an abstract adversarial
game. We are but its instruments,

paid to deliver only evidence:
smoking guns and bodies:
facts in lieu of truth.

In such a system there can be
only dead or man-handled victims;
a man is a man, whatever he does.

What he has done must be proven
beyond a reasonable doubt. And
knowledge *comes* with a high price.

We tried to catch him in the act;
we followed him even into his dreams:
we are none the wiser, don't you see?

A man who can pound a spike
in a little boy's head
is not going to blanch at anything said.

Such a man sleeps well, has no conscience
to disturb, however many holes we punch
in the lid of the jar we keep him in.
And so the system pays for the bodies.
And so the lawyers for the family members
must try to reclaim what is rightfully theirs

while we stick him in stir
with a pair of scissors
to cut out paper dolls,

unfold them gently
so the children can hold hands again
and circle us in a fairy ring

and ring around the rosy aureole of truth
with their pockets emptied of posies
until — husha, husha — they all fall down

gentle as the down
that once filled their pillows,
give our thoughts at last
the rule of gravity to cling to again.

6. *Final Reprise: The Victims*

Go easy now, we will see you anon.
And pray for Clifford and all the others
whose will is not their own to bend
to a purpose that would suit you.
What is done is done; we are undone
only as gold threads in an old garment,
and he and all the other killers
whose lust only knew a black purpose,
are but black threads in the same fabric.
What he wanted he took from us,
but what we were able to give could not
slake his thirst. Say only that he traded
notoriety for fame   and bought a piece
of the same real estate we must all
pay for in the end. Say only that such evil
is the consequence of taking what could not
be freely given. That he came to this pass
by slow degrees, and so showed us a dark side
to the planets of our being. His will
a speeding electron shot down the short
barrel of a cyclotron of hate, shattered
the closely-knit molecules of all our lives
only for a moment, the way a rock shatters
the surface of a still pond, the way the atom
bombs dropped on Hiroshima and Nagasaki
broke the surface of a bigger pond and
sent out ripples that would sound our depths
and seek the nether limits of our shores.

And though you say he should be consigned to
hell for his deeds, and we are in heaven now,
none of us is the wiser for our metaphors,
and there is no sky to understanding
we might reach but that defined
by the clay that clings to our feet.
Do with him what you must;
we are already at peace,
inasmuch as air can breathe
life into dust.

AFTER YOUR DIVORCE

After your divorce
you walk along the shoreline;
each step a fresh wound
forces the water ahead,
fills a dry socket behind.

DOING A PROCESS

Think, for a moment, of a toilet. Imagine it's clean, if it makes it any easier. That's it. Now, imagine this is the first toilet you've ever seen. Imagine you are Thomas Crapper and this is the prototype toilet. Forget for a moment whether there's a chain or a handle to flush it. Imagine it as it exists now. It's your toilet; you invented it. It can be white, pink, baby blue — whatever colour you like. It's your toilet. I'll say it's white.

Notice its perfect lustre. The way light plays off its perfect curved porcelain finish. There's not a chip in it. Not a crack. No one's taken a shotgun to this one to see if it would crack when he flushed it. It's perfect. White and whole as a store-bought egg. Cleaner, brighter. You can hardly look at it it's so bright. And yet you must. There is something about it. A certain *je ne sais quoi*. Being the first toilet, it carries no burden of prior association. It is priceless, exquisite as a Ming vase. Is of such a port in air that you imagine you are looking into the seamless corolla of the world's first flower. Its beauty astounds you. You stand speechless before it. Stare at the limpid pool of water and see yourself restored, whole. The reflection is perfect. The water is perfectly still. Not so much as a hair displaces it.

Now relax. Let your eyes travel around the inside of the bowl. Feel it with your eyes. Imagine you are a fly. Each sense — sight, touch, smell, taste, hearing, the high gear of extrasensory perception — is engaged, lingers like the leg of a fly in that instant when it first makes contact with the porcelain. Each sensation is perfect. Each sensation knows no bounds. Having no boundaries, no one sensation is distinct from the next. There is only the sensation of wholeness, perfection. No sense of the mind containing it.

This is the first toilet and the last toilet. Your eyes have backed off from any and every part of it. You see the whole toilet. Nothing but the toilet. It glows, holds your complete attention. Having invented it for some particular function, you have completely forgotten for the moment what that function is. Beauty and function have become one and you are speechless before *it*.

This thing, this toilet does not yet have a name. You tremble with excitement before it the way you would before a perfect piece of quartz or a semi-precious stone a wave has suddenly revealed in the eternal, diurnal wash of the sea. It is a moon snail not yet recognized as such. A strange, alien thing. You feel its power come over you even as you feel powerful for having created it. The hum of its electrons contain you and you it. All of your molecules are humming to the same tune, as though your body were a giant tuning fork struck by the mallet of its perfection.

Now you see yourself take hold of the rim of the bowl. You are gripping both sides of the bowl. Your hands are in the position of ten to two on the steering wheel of an immense truck. All the muscles in your body are completely relaxed. You can feel yourself getting very sleepy. Your head slumps forward on the wheel. All directions have become one direction. There is a smell of lilac. It is as though you have just bent forward to smell the full spray of the lilac blossoms after a spring shower. You are lost in the whirl of electrons that is each tiny bud. There is only the one sense and that is the smell of lilac.

Were there any other sense you could not help but notice it. The whiteness of your arms, face. The way a strand of your hair falls forward, only just touches the surface of the water like a willow leaf. How your reflection jerks like a water strider caught on the tensile surface at the edge of your left eye. How slowly, surely, a line of sputtum slides down your chin like a snail on the world's first leaf. How a slow-forming pendant of blood begins to descend down your lip. How it gathers in the little trench at the base of the septum. At the precise juncture the angels put their thumbprint upon you when you were born.

How a shudder like the shudder of tailfeathers comes over you when the angels walk across your grave. How a hand reaches for the world's first lever. The first shaker of salt.

TO THE GIRL WHO DID HANDSPRINGS
AT OUR WEDDING RECEPTION

My father chugs around the dance floor
like the little engine that could,
shouts, "Give me a rhumba!
Give me a rhumba!"

My mother grows silent and sullen.
Wishes he couldn't
and wouldn't
chuff his way through every number.

My brother too is in his cups
and does a fast tai chi
through "I'm turning Japanese,
I think I'm turning Japanese. . . ."

The Vapors. Post-punk.
He wears his tie as a sweatband,
thinks this dance is his
last kata with chance;
has forgotten, he doesn't dance.

Nobody does; no one's in control.
Not Joe's mother-in-law,
who's lost control of her bladder
and is oblivious to the sodden
tea bag of her panty hose,

not the relatives,
the only ones to notice.
Least of all the girl in jeans
from off the street
who asks politely for booze
and does cartwheels for free.

No one, that is, except some
old guy on the parking lot
who wants to talk to someone in charge.
"Take me to your leader," he says.
Strange, remote —

like the disgruntled Venusian in the joke
who has to tell his captain
he's failed to communicate
with the gas pump
he takes to be a human being.

"No wonder. He can't hear you,"
his captain proclaims,
looking out for a moment on
the lonely Hopper street scene.
"He's got his dick in his ear!"

Only this guy says,
"I don't mind her dancing
if she's not disturbing you,
but, please, don't let her drink.
She's just got out of the hospital.
She's on medication."

Meaning: she's on Librium,
has tripped a few switches
before lighting up the control
panel of this spacecraft,
and that it's late.
Too late for any of us to beam down.

Yet she has the presence of mind
to disappear, return in a dress
before her father returns to collect her.
Is young and sweet
as only dancing girls in dresses can be.

So sweet that,
of all the details about her,
I remember best
the floral pattern of her dress,
her shy manner the next day
when I passed her enroute to the hall.

She wouldn't look up and acknowledge me
until I raised a finger from the
steering wheel and winked.
The life of our party she was too:
a young girl no one knew!

A young woman who skipped
and did another little dance,
as if this were hopscotch
and she were going to
stand on one foot,
bend over to pick up her marker.

The same marker that makes
my heart do a little jig
when I watch my daughter
skip and jump that way —
now, a full ten years later.

A stone that says,
"The party may be over,
but I'm still here."
Or: "Ground control to Major Tom:
I've got my earth boots on.
Wanna dance? Mind if I
do a cartwheel across your lawn?"

A stone that may be
the original omphalos:
the belly button of the world
— or something I forgot
to take out of my ear.

ULTRASOUND, EIGHT WEEKS

So strange, so seemingly inhuman
at this stage, you might be
an undulating or peristaltic wave
of some mottled mollusk's mantle
seen in extreme close-up;
or, even closer, as if magnified
by electron microscope, a tiny
mitochondrion or other organelle
responsible for nourishing the cell.
But no: this tiny palpitating dot,
this seed seen in cross-section
through the womb, is you: our son,
little minnow obscured beneath
the vast undinal wave of the sea
and we, two fishermen,
pitched and tossed
between peak and trough
of your tiny heartbeat's
electrocardiograph,
are receiving your faint
blip on our sonar,
so you cannot swim through our
fine, reticulated
net of new emotions.
But you do.
You appear and disappear
like an octopus or squid behind
your own inky jet expulsion
and force us to seek
a rapprochement requiring
a re-shifting of the continental plates
to get you back in focus, dredge you up.

And I wonder what slack-jawed
cabezon or aquanaut you will
finally turn out to be
and whether or not
you will swallow your own tail
the way this miracle swallows us,
the screen's glass pseudopod
of love threatening to bud off,
and, like a medusa or hydra,
go your separate, salty way
before you even get here,
splash down. Love is suddenly
that minute and focussed;
the feeling after first seeing you
that huge.

CRADLE PICTURE
(for Christian)

Three days old in the picture,
eyes closed, you pucker
your mouth around something
the camera's peristalsis
catches now in my throat
like a tiny fishbone.

I can see the sky
blue as a toy bear
repeated endlessly,
symmetrically
over the page
as it is on your blanket.

I want to tell you
silence is measured
in fisherman's inches,
the breadth of your arms
will contain
the words that get away.

Your gesture of oration
is complete now,
vaguely shaped like
the letter 'O' in
my mind.

It is an oval portrait
you keep open
with your hands.

THE SCAR

One scar — no more than a slight discolouration of the skin between the last three toes of my daughter's right foot. I hadn't really noticed it until she started running naked through the back sprinkler and started getting her second tan. For some reason this small patch doesn't tan — quite. And now it comes back to me: a reminder of the time she kicked the hot water over while I was making her bottle. She was six months old; this scar, doubtless, the first of many she will receive. Yet the sight of it sears like a hot brand into my own flesh just seeing it now. Knowing something perfect — a miracle that has been given to me and my wife for safekeeping — is as fragile as the tattered epidermis I see again hanging from her scalded foot — scars me yet again somehow. And I see that her pride at being able to splash around in the backyard wading pool has given her scar a life of its own. How animate it is! Like a leaf-shaped nudibranch pulsating with life. The water shimmers and it wiggles, writhes, seems to ride the currents with her. And when she slides out of the pool and shivers and drips on the walkway, it is as though the first amphibian were somehow trying out its own newly-grown limbs. It glistens too. Draws my eye to it as surely as the green jewel of a frog draws to it a young prince's kiss. So that one day she might be a princess and have her own castle of flesh to hide in. Her own keloid narrative or fairy tale to grow pearls of memory around. I kiss it now and wait for the day.

"GOKE"
for Marika

"Goke? Birdy goke?" you ask,
your own voice seeking a kind
of updraught on the final syllable
of your own newly acquired wings.

And, "Yes, honey, the bird's neck
is broken. Birdy's dead," we reply.
The birdy flew into our window.
It saw the trees. It tried to land.
Went boom and fell. Birdy all gone now."

"Goke," you reply with certainty,
and stroke its feathers fondly.
" 'Sis? 'Sis?" you want to know.
"This is its beak, honey. Beak."
And this, for the moment at least,
seems to satisfy you. You smile.

The bird is definitely goke.

PEEKABOO

Adrian is intent as Mom turns the page,
Sucks at his first bottle of the day.
He has his fingers on all the stops
of the sassiest saxophone
ever to play a blue note.
Is poised to pour
pure ambrosia into our ears.
So hip he can blow a cornucopia
of imagined notes, string them out
crisp as white linen on a line,
or hold each note firm and round
as an iridescent soap bubble,
rotate it on its own surface tension
until it breaks free,
perfectly formed to defy gravity.
Only this is serious business.
He frowns, leans over the words.
Where's Mommy? Peekaboo!
Where's Daddy? Peekaboo!
Mom intones as she turns
each carefully hinged page.
Jack-in-the-box characters pop up
to play his and hers solos from behind
first a bedsheet, then a newspaper.
Terribly strange business this.
The enigmatic black letters
of each perfectly formed word
dress against each other
like troops on parade.
You don't say? Adrian's eyes
seem to ask in reply.

You mean these little squiggles
actually tell you what noises to make?
Who'd've guessed it!
Peekaboo, that's it?
Pop up and smile, say your name?
Hot damn, that's somethin'!
What does a guy have to do
to get a refill around here?
Salute? Reallllly wail?
Wrap your minds around this . . .
Tell me if you've heard
this tune before.

NEW BLACK SHOES
for Marika

Gangway grannies! Heads up grandpas!
Single moms with sullen broods in tow,
Christmas shoppers with coin slots for mouths
unstitch your brows, open Al Jolson eyes.

Marika's got new black patent leather shoes!
Is a bowling ball rolling clickety clack
down the mall. Nothing short of a potted palm
will stop her. She smiles in each shiny toe.

She doesn't need to click her heels thrice
and repeat "There's no place like home"
to get from Oz to wherever she's going,
and this sure as hell ain't Kansas!

Planets, whole galaxies of Christmas lights
gleam back from those toes. "I'm Dorfy, Mom.
I'm Dorfy!" she exclaims. Look at me go!
The wizard, whatsisname's got nothing on me.

So who cares if he's off on a coffee break
and none of his photo-taking elves are on seat?
This ain't Oz or the North Pole, but I've got
black patent leather shoes. I'm Dorfy. I'm me.

SHHH, THEY'RE SLEEPING

The old Singer had not been used
for anything but a plant stand
when our daughter commandeered it.
Now its six little drawers are crypts,
Murphy beds for dinosaurs.
The Stegosaurus sleeps in one,
The Tyrannosaurus Rex in another,
Triceratops in a third, and so on:
each carefully molded out of play dough
and left to fossilize in Kleenex swaddling.

A nice touch is the short strings she ties
to each little knob, the switchboard
linkage from one drawer to another.
Now it's as though a telephone operator
had given us a direct line from Plasticene
to Pleistocene. We not only share
a planet's reserves of bondable carbon atoms,
but a party line with the crusty old folks
of the Upper Cretaceous. *Shhh*, Marika says
whenever we stray too close. *They're sleeping*.

On a molecular level, we like to think
she may be right. Who knows what sediment
the fluorocarbon layer and exhaust emissions,
spent fossil fuels, and paving are laying down
in the form of fallout from recombinant atoms?
All we can do is pussyfoot around the playroom.
Listen to the roots of each potted plant
as they suck up nutrients like the last
quarter-inch of some teenager's vanilla shake.
Tramp down years of sediment everywhere we walk.

RETURN OF THE SON OF SOYA SAUCE

I've got some bad news for you
my wife says as I come through the door.
Your VCR's ground to a halt.

I think, great; isn't that always the way:
you get through all the turnstiles
of another week, and something breaks.

Just when I'd begun to look forward
to putting my feet up. Suddenly *I'm*
in a bad movie, thrust into the bad guy role.

I'm unable to control the horizontal
or the vertical; I have no remote control,
no fast forward, no reverse mode.

I feel an old rage cue up inside me —
as if my wife had turned me on
and shoved a tape into my mouth.

Can see myself spouting vituperative
lines of how nothing's built to last,
short circuiting on ozone sparks of blame.

Cartoon gouts of smoke pour out of my ears,
my face contorts in paroxysms of hate;
I become the son of something from outer space

or a cyborg with a dud circuit board
or defective chip. My polypropelene skin
melts to reveal my circuitry.

I think: toaster . . . microwave . . . computer.
Adrian's seen me insert cassettes into drives
so many times to serve up entertainment,

he's decided to plug something in by himself.
A cheese sandwich maybe. Or Duplo blocks,
in the hope that some building might come up

on the screen. That the world I've made for him
will suddenly display itself in VGA pixels.
That a cheese sandwich will shout Dolby sound.

I rant and rave through all the old tapes
of I-told-you-sos, pick-this-ups, put-that-aways,
what-do-you-do-all-days, until I'm exhausted —

as if I could scrunch the whole world up
like a bag and thrust it into a pneumatic chute
to be whisked somewhere beyond this mad circuitry.

As if the whole sky were littered with crumbs
that somehow ended up on my carpet just after I'd
vacuumed the place. Or some miracle might occur.

My missing socks, lost in the Twilight Zone,
might materialize, come tumbling out of the VCR.
Hang, perfect notes, on staves of the known universe.

I'd become the wild-haired maestro of a new music
that would rival the tuning of the spheres, snap
all five senses back into harmony. Just like that.

I'm so righteous, I'm going to fix that damn VCR
at midnight, before I turn into Mr. Hyde, or pay
some jerk a fortune to remove that cheese sandwich.

So I start unscrewing screws, remove the sleeve,
and — lo and behold — I'm right! There they sit:
two cello packs of soya sauce. All my spleen

contained. Unbroken packets of castor oil
left over from my childhood. Glistening jewels.
I'm Doctor Jekyll. All sweetness and light.

I scrub to begin surgery. Put on rubber gloves
of reason and hope. "Forceps," I say and begin
to remove the implants of forty years of male rage.

TELEFOMIN TROUSERS
for Don & Susan Low

Whoever thought of the name
had his head screwed on right.
Imagine the ad campaign
that could be built around
these two alliterative words:
"All the best Third World people
are wearing them this season . . . .
Feel the sea breeze in your hair,
let it caress your derriere."

The four syllables of the adjective
suggest a picturesque village
in the Shetlands or Orkneys,
some Atlantic rookery
buffeted by wind, celebrated for
the fine homespun wool
of its dour-faced sheep.

Telefomin, Telefomin . . . .
You can hear a thick brogue,
practically see some old guy's
moustache come up dripping with foam
as he bangs the table with his
empty pint of Guinness
or Thistle brand stout.

Aye, and there lies a tale
in the choice of noun too.
So proper, so serious:
we're talking British flannel here —
By Appointment to Her Majesty,
the Queer Old Dean. Designer label
in a pair of Carnaby slacks
with creases so sharp
they could slice cheese.

But no. These trousers are not
tailored from the finest wool
or polyester dacron,
but are grown; nay, grow wild,
are hand-picked from the vine
in Telefomin, New Guinea,
and aren't trousers at all!

Indeed, if I wasn't told otherwise,
I would have thought these
Peter Pan gourds with their
elfin curlicue tips were
powder horns, or at least
were used to store some
aphrodisiac or herbal emetic.
The thong of binder twine glued
beneath the thatched band of grass
might be worn over the shoulder.

Instead, this thingamabob is worn
over the penis. The binder twine
fits around the waist;
the gentle curve of the gourd
is worn up, between the legs,
like Peter Pan's winkle pickers
or Alladin's Scheherazade slippers.

Thus, there is no need of guessing
the extent of a man's wealth.

You have to laugh when you think
of grown men traipsing around the jungle
like that. With not a stitch on
but their Telefomin Trousers. You do
when you tell me the tale. I do
as I gaze in amazement at the souvenir
on my study wall. And yet a man might
liberally sprinkle a kind of moondust
from this little cornucopia too.

Imagine the men of our society
wearing them instead of pants.
How the Peter Pan curve might restore
a kind of innocence to members
that long to poke their heads
over waistbands like Kilroys
with wide eyes and little 'o' mouths.
And think then of the codpiece:
the cup that made much ado of nothing
and hid whatever the little guy
kept tucked inside his leotards.

Maybe if Adam had been issued
a pair of Telefomin Trousers,
Eden would not have become
a designer or sex boutique
but something more akin to
a trick and joke shop
where you might buy condoms
that fit like a night cap
instead of the nylon stocking
or ski mask a cat burglar wears.

All our men — dingled or donged —
could pretend to be Peter Pan,
and take Wendy and the kids —
with or without nightshirts
out the bedroom window
for a spin around the neighbourhood.
We could stud our Telefomin Trousers
with beadwork and jewels,
instead of our scabbards.
We could put up our bright swords.

Think of it! In less than a decade
we might replace the points of our missiles
with delicate curves. The older they are
the more curved we could make them:
ram's horns poking out of every silo.
great architectural thing poems that followed
the aesthetic of the Fibonacci sequence
and sat there for all to wonder at
like Nautilus shells dragged from
some briny deep of the unconscious.

Even men's penises might evolve into
sea cucumber-like organs, party favours
that ended in a feathery flick
instead of a bald head and Simonized shine.
Might come alive, mouths agape
like birds in their nests,
rather than rise like heat-seaking missiles
from silos deep beneath hopsack or denim.
If only we wore Telefomin Trousers,
trained our little pickles
to stretch for the light.

REBCON II ™

Six hundred dollars
my wife paid for this car:
a '55 Morris Oxford,
the first thing she saw with four wheels
after she got off the plane.
Two years in Africa will do that to you.
No hubcaps, calico-spotted with primer and Bond-o:
a cute little beast in obvious need of a home —
something to get dewy-eyed, anthropomorphic about.
Call it a laughing hyena;
it saw her coming, if its trainer didn't.
They were meant for each other.

The trunk wouldn't lock,
so thieves promptly relieved us of our tools,
and the windshield wipers — hydraulic —
were never really very good when they worked —
wouldn't so much as whisk away my tears when I
first beheld her spotted flanks in the drive.
But never fear! Sears has the solution on sale!
Rebcon II, the new miracle spray. Just buff
with a dry cloth — whoosh — no need of wipers:
water spatters into mercuric beads,
dances off the windshield as off a hot griddle!

So here we are:
caught in the worst downpour
since I got back from the monsoons.
Screaming down the freeway
at 100 kilometers per,
and she sounds like a Drummond twin-prop
about to leave this earth.

Four lanes of traffic
headed into Vancouver.
This is it! This is it!
I'm not even going to get
to kiss my own keister goodbye,
let alone swap spit with the Missus!

But for once in my life
the commercials don't lie!
Thumpity thump and rat-a-tat-tat:
take that, the rain says,
and it's true: if we were in
a gangster movie right now,
we'd be swiss cheeze;
old Morris's exhaust pipe
would be hanging
like a cigarette from the curled lip
of some sleek Chevy's sardonic grill —

But wait! The stuff flies
off us like welding sparks!
God's given us a break!
I am truly amazed that this car
that might have come over on Noah's Arc
is saved by a few eye drops
administered to the windows of her soul!
Suddenly this boxy clunker's
slick as a lozenge.
We're in the Deas Island tunnel,
can literally feel
the peristaltic waves of God's grace
working us through the system.

I want to sing hallelujah!
Praise British engineers everywhere
for the pleasure of smelling mildew
and musty leather seats.
Rebcon II — migawd!
What it might do for my own pipes,
and still I'm twitchy,
pull four yards of cotton
out of the seat, just sitting there,
hands at ten to two on the steering wheel.

Maybe this isn't the Deas Island tunnel.
Maybe this is the real pooper shoot:
the tunnel to the afterlife.
We're in the Twilight Zone,
have not quite crossed over.
Instead of harp music,
we've got Ray Coniff
seeping like a gas from the dash.

We're shuffling off this mortal coil
in a '55 Morris,
and my wife is saying,
"I told you so! I told you so!
Oh ye of little faith!
If God had wanted us
to have windshield wipers,
he'd have seen these worked
as cleanly as a wipe
across the camera lens.
Each time the wipers came down
he'd have restored
a new vista of Eden.

The dotted line would have been
solid and double."
Still, I wonder: each drop is big,
fat as water off a duck's ass. **Rebcon II** . . .
What a bald man could do with such stuff,
singin' in the rain: See Ma! No hat!
Hair is what God gave baby apes
to cling to before there were toupees . . .
We're in the breach position —
coming through on a day
as sunny as any in heaven.

ABOUT THE AUTHOR

Richard Stevenson is the author of four previous full-length collections of poetry: *Driving Offensively* (Sono Nis Press, 1985), *Suiting Up* (Third Eye Publications, 1986), *Horizontal Hotel* (TSAR Publications, 1989), and *Whatever It Is Plants Dream...* (Goose Lane Editions, 1990); and four chapbooks: *Hierarchy At the Feeder* (1984) and *Twelve Houseplants* (1985), both from Pierian Press/dollarpoem editions; and *Dick and Jane Have Sex* (Greensleeve Publications, 1990), and *A Dog Called Normal* (Egorag Press, forthcoming). A past Editor-in-Chief of *Prism international* and founding editor of *Black Apple*, he currently lives with his wife Gepke and two children, Adrian and Marika, in Lethbridge, Alberta, and teaches English, Humanities, Technical and Creative Writing courses for Lethbridge Community College.